Crown Jewels

ISBN-13: 978-0-9914332-0-9
ISBN-10: 0-9914332-0-3

First printing, April, 2014

Illustrations by Rosemary C. Gray

Crown photos used on front cover, back cover and second title page by Scanrail (Oleksiy Mark)

Cover design by ThomasMax

Published by:

 ThomasMax Publishing
P.O. Box 250054
Atlanta, GA 30325
www.thomasmax.com

Crown Jewels

Poetry by
Judith Barban

Judith Barban (signature)

Illustrated by Rosemary C. Gray

ThomasMax

Your Publisher
For The 21st Century

For my sisters Frances and Claire,
and my husband Gene,
and especially
for Mary and Frank, my parents

Crown Jewels

Crowns

I wore a crown of gold
to walk through the streets
and as I walked I grew
taller and taller so tall
I could not see my feet

I wore a crown of thorns
to trudge up the mountain
and as I trudged blood ran
down my cheeks and arms
until it filled my palms

I wore a crown of simple cloth
to sit in a silent room
and as I waited in the dark
loneliness came
and sat beside me

I wore a crown of sugar pops
to distribute at the fair
red blue orange and green
children laughed
and thought I was a clown

I wore a crown of love
to stroll through the garden
and as I strolled the scent
of lilacs filled the air
and sparrows nested in my hair

I
Antique Jewelry:
Remembrance of Things Past

Love in the Sixties

I

We smoke first,
holding it hot in out throats,
waiting for freedom.
Hair so soft—his long, mine longer—
gently wisping on our cheeks
spurs the senses
so we make love not war.
Within the circle of defeated time
we move liberated and loving
as though through this act we end
the war and children crying and animals dying
and imagine a paradise on earth.

We speak in solemn smiles after,
vaguely thinking of next time
—if there should be—
(I'm glad your eyes just missed mine)
and part more hollow than before.

Love in the Sixties

II

I seek an answer in the stars
study my open palm
flee the past, take refuge in the future
Yet the firmament is bounded by you
filled with planets of once-known love
and meteors of remembered moments
that crash without warning
on the surface of my heart

(My fingers brush your forearm
It is summer. *The first touch*)

I move quietly in the void you left
believing your return
every footstep yours
every call your voice

(They leave us alone, the music loud
I touch your hair. Autumn. *The second*)

Days have passed, months perhaps
Orion descends
I am worn
weary with mourning
But I shall wait my love
and find you
someday
in a galaxy across the universe

Soul Music

For the first time
I have counted time
a strange rhythm
a novel tune
played in tear-shaped notes
strung across life's measured staff
in bars of days and nights
a melody of loneliness and loss
the battle hymn
of the human heart

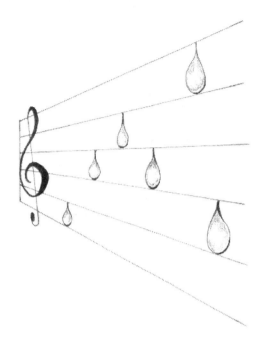

Between

An ocean swells between us,
we are two continents divided.
But did I not discern on your horizon
the flagship of a smile?

A lake lies between us.
Shall we hoist our sails
and let the winds of inclination
carry us off shore?

A river runs between us,
the boundaries of our lands are set.
But have I not in small moments
dug out a canoe of confidences?

A stream shallows between us.
Now reach across and steady me—
There, I've taken off my shoes—
I love to wade, don't you?

Mack from Texas
a graduate student at Emory University in 1962

One night you drove
non-stop from Miami
to type my term paper
due the next day
to be with me—
I saw the joy on your face
when you rushed in
You typed, I proofed
When you pulled the last page
from the Olivetti
you opened a bottle of Tia Maria
took a swallow
drew me close
kissed me pouring the liqueur
from your mouth into mine
yet I felt nothing
but the sweet liquid on my tongue

If

if there were a place
where one could plant and grow
and not lay waste
the only pain a mother's labor
the only death nature's reclaiming
those who have stopped dreaming

if there were a place
where men could understand
and never hate
a paradise of peace
each taking the other's hand
knowing each is free

if there were a place
where love could come
to stop awhile
and rest from all
her weary cycles
it would be here

my cheek against your shoulder
in the warmth of naked sleep
while in our dreams
the other places
if they could be
would be

On the Beach

I watch
a little girl
in shallow waves
dipping her bucket
pouring sea water
on her tiny feet
sun and wind
in baby blond hair
pure light
in pure eyes
once
I was
that little girl
laughing I ran
to mother
waiting on the sand
she wrapped me
in a sun-warmed towel
folded me
in love-warmed arms

I watch
knowing
one day she will be
like me
seeing and remembering
a little girl
and her bucket
on the beach

High School Reunions

The early ones we
are married
have jobs
have kids
girls look good
boys have bellies
and thinning hair
we're drinking
too many cocktails
laughing too loud
dancing old style
we promise
to stay in touch

Middle ones we
look at pictures
of a few who've passed
share problems of
work, finances, health
we're talking too much
about our children's
lives and not our own
don't dance much
don't drink much
exchange email
and promise
to stay in touch

Later ones we
smile a lot
some use canes
one in a wheelchair
no longer mention
all who've passed
glad to be here

quiet conversations
about simple hobbies
look at pictures of
grandchildren and
their kids
hope and pray
to stay in touch

Sitting on the Screen Porch Sipping Ice Tea

Sitting on the screen porch sipping ice tea
sacred temple, holy wine
haven of rest
for the mind, for the soul
water for my southern roots
no thoughts
no planning
just listening
to the flutter of passing wings
the silence of passing clouds
the cycle of nature

Barefoot wearing short shorts
and a halter top
despite the crooked toes
varicose veins
and sagging breasts
feeling
the breeze on my face
the simple joy of being
the peace that passes understanding
just the same as
when I was a teen

the tea tastes the same
the *me* is the same
I guess there are
some things
that never change like
sitting on the screen porch sipping ice tea

Moments

moments
picked by memory
peaks and valleys
whatever is sharp
stabbing stinging
pain
whatever is a rush of
unexpected
joy

highs and lows
stored 'till the end
of the functioning
brain

everyday moments
slowly wrapped in
layers of gauze
are discarded
like yesterday's
newspaper

II
Family Jewels:
Ties That Bind the Heart

Vallie Claire

one summer
every afternoon
lying in cross-breezes
of the back bedroom
you read to me
The Mystery of Carlotta
opened a new world
of haciendas and fiestas
sombreros and sarapes
I cried at the end
because it was the end

when friends came
to play in the yard
you made up games
gave us new names
roused us with
your imagination
that transformed
the ordinary into
a magic kingdom

on Saturdays
you took me
to the movies
and held my hand
throughout the film
protected me from
celluloid monsters
bought me popcorn
and licorice candy

Today I thought
of your name
in French
vallée claire
how you were
the bright sister
in the shadow of
my childhood valley

Daddy

I saw the sun-gold of his hair
turn to the silver of moonlight
(my days will not number so many
nor my fortune so kindly fare)
he perhaps does not know
how much he has shared
nor perhaps how much I have cared

Through yellowed albums, brass buttons
old bullets, and trinkets he has told
the adventures of many years past
created visions of plows and peace
of wanderings and war
a boy on the farm, a young man at sea
these he has been

Yet for me he will always be
a hand holding a child's hand
while she dreamed of storybook animals
an office to visit with calendar moons to cut
a garden to plant, a cat to feed
daughters to raise, a house to heat
a lesson in nature's way
of things growing and green
of the ultimate return, calm and serene
to the final dream, the final sleep

Road Trips Used to Be Fun

road trips used to be fun
two-lane blacktops
making you wonder
what's over the hill
getting stuck behind a farmer's truck
then waving as you pass
carrying your own thermos jug
of sweet ice tea with lemon slices
poured into paper cups
at a wayside picnic table
ham sandwiches on white bread
no lettuce or tomato just mayo

Daddy at the wheel, Mama beside him
us Kids in the back
feeling the breeze
from the open front windows
playing car games like
the number of cows on your side
or naming animals that start
with each letter of the alphabet
I always got the q and x
singing, sleeping, singing again

the destination wasn't foremost in our minds
we just enjoyed the journey

Getting a New Dog

we haven't had a dog
since our golden retriever passed
eight years ago
the grief passed
not the memories
they float around, surface from time to time
shining colored
bubbles in the sun
we can talk about him now and smile
it's time

to get a new dog
but what about
the time the work the money
but what about
the love the company the joy
okay but what breed
we buy books
look at pictures
of each kind
we discuss the pros and cons
of different ones
from teacup poodle to great dane
long and shorthair
pointed ears or floppy
we argue and pace
disagree and insist

to pick a pup
we get in the car
and drive to the pound

Family Reunion

I met her at the Santee River
aunts, uncles, cousins galore
gathered for the occasion
but she was none of these
she must have been about six or seven
pretty close to my same age
one of my cousins said
she lived down the dirt road
that ran off the highway
near their fishing cabin

While grown-ups sat on the porch
drinking beer or lemonade
talking about uninteresting things
she asked me if I wanted to play
house in the fish-cleaning shed
that stood close to the water

We sat on overturned buckets
in the damp gray place
snapping twigs as if they were
green beans pretending rocks
were potatoes in this house
this little home of our own

She had the brightest eyes
dark pearls on white satin
her smile a flash of pure light
she gave me bouquets of laughter
and placed them in my heart

"Please, Daddy, can't we
take her home with us?"
Time to go, car doors shut
she stood barefoot on the gravel
a shy one-handed wave goodbye
tears shining on her smooth black skin

Three Christmas Trees

seventy-five Christmases celebrated
meld into one and the same
except for three trees

the live spruce tall and full
decorated with golden garlands
sheltered piles of presents for all
while we kids sang carols
and Mom and Dad drank eggnog

the discount-store artificial fir
barely fit into a corner
of our first apartment home
the star at the top
shining its lovelight
on two packages and two hearts

now this one maybe a foot high
covered with tiny silver balls
my grandson brought it
when they came to visit
it's enough for me alone
and tomorrow
if my knees are not too bad
I will place it on your grave

There Was a Time

there was a time when

life was nothing but just having fun
there were never any errands to run

every day we played in the yard
and didn't have to work real hard

using our wits we invented new games
without thinking of our future aims

we were doctors and nurses, even movie stars
no mortgages to pay for houses and cars

we made a princess out of the kitty
never thought to form a committee

knowing that soon we'd be eating spaghetti
we didn't have to get dinner ready

running and jumping with energy galore
no complaining that muscles were sore

we were all so eager to be grown
our innocent minds could not have known

III
Uncut Gemstones:
The Natural World

Seasonal Haiku

<u>Fall</u> (a Liturgical haiku)

> Grapes ripe on the vine
> pray to be the sacrifice—
> Eucharistic wine.

<u>Winter</u>

> Dead leaves from the oak,
> lying frozen under snow,
> crack beneath my boot.

> Blackbirds on the wire,
> halfway there, from who knows where,
> rest awhile in flight.

<u>Spring</u>

> Little heads lift up;
> crocuses and daffodils
> promise us the sun.

<u>Summer</u>

> Corn, ready to shuck,
> would wave its golden tassel,
> but the air is still.

The Locusts of Summer in the South

Rigid, immobilized
affixed to the bark
of a red oak
with shrill vibrations
they sing in anticipation
of liberation from
their petrified prison shells
fevered vibratos that rise and fall
like a spirited choir
singing a hymn of praise.

Some call them cicadas
but it really doesn't matter
the important thing is
they come out of their hard shells
emerging new, with delicate wings
to fly away
like we will do
at the Resurrection
at least that's what
I learned as a child
in Sunday School

I've Learned

I've learned to
recognize the birds
that come
to my feeders
in some species
I can distinguish
male from female
young from old

I know
their calls
what seeds
each prefers
which suet cake
for that season

I know
when hummingbirds
arrive and depart
how much sugar
what color
to make their water

I've learned to
stop the squirrels
from stealing
but let them
have a drink
from the bath
and sometimes
put out peanuts

my doctorate of
philosophy
did not teach me
these essential things
I've learned them
in the settle
and slow
of retirement years

Feeder Wars

you sit there mocking me
it glints in your eye
your tail propped against your back
in a defiant question mark

See? Crisco on the pole doesn't work

your greasy rodent paws
folded in a false gassho
hold a sunflower seed
stolen from my squirrel-proof feeder

keeping an eye on me
you nibble
your cheeks fast like a rabbit's
only not so innocent

trapeze artist that you are
you can leap on it
hang upside down on it
swing on it bounce on it

finishing your purloined meal
you rat-hop along the railing
give me a final glance
then sip from their bath water

Okay, you win this time

I turn from the window
furrow my brow
open the pantry door
and plan my next maneuver

2013: The Summer of No Sun

every morning
hoping
I open the blinds
gray sky again

it drifts down
menacing
covers my brain
in its filmy gauze

I plod about
feeling
down and out
in my spirit now

I do things
going
through the motions
of my daily chores

by noon the rain is
starting
by late July
no " maybe tomorrow"

Virus

I don't even know
what you look like
no doubt
you're horribly ugly
how dare you
steal your way
into my nose, throat, and lungs
to reek havoc

I'd like to spray you
with Raid
watch you die
a painful death
like a cockroach or spider
on your back
legs flailing the air
gasping for breath
like me

I'm calling forth the troops
of red and white corpuscles
hot soup and tea
aspirin and vitamin C
bed rest and TV
lozenges for the throat
syrup for the cough
Nyquil for my sleep

but if you hang on
my secret weapon
will do you in
just you wait and see
a frothy cup of hot chocolate
with mini marshmallows
slowly melting on top

Out West

sandstone shapes
bits and pieces of change
sculpted by wind
stand like markers

sharp peaks
rows of white pavilions
a shock against the blue
push skyward

native mysteries
carved in cliffs
stubbornly resist
the archeologist's pick

canyon walls
deep as inferno
cast slow shadows
on earth's striations

visitors' centers
Indian curio shops
western wear and rodeos
draw the tourist crowd

who buy moccasins
and dream-catchers
try cowboy hats
and silver-buckled belts

then sit out front
on picnic benches
sharing snacks
with restless kids

some just speed by
cameras at the window
while country Jesus
plays on the car radio

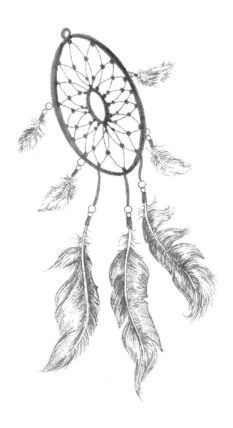

Sea Poem

we search for sand dollars
at the ocean's edge
that ever-changing, rolling
deposits them as it recedes
some broken some almost full
there in the shallow water
a whole one
promise of luck
symbol of faith
gift from the sea
but oh
for every treasure brought
the many taken away

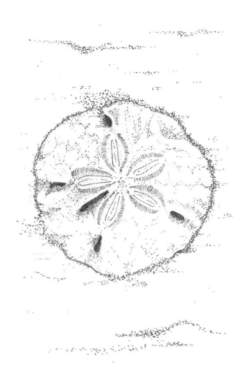

Dirge

the moon died tonight
no globe or crescent
to arch its way through stars
no light
to thread through wooded paths
no silver
to shimmer on darkened waters
no beams
to get in childrens' eyes
and make them dream
their fantasy lives
no guide
for sailors, lovers,
wayfarers or wolves
no gleam
through our bedroom window
and though I prop up on one elbow
I cannot see your sleeping face

Broken Branch

After the storm
A maple limb on the lawn
Is dragged off
To some forsaken place

The unbalanced tree
Extends the stub
Upward as if
To prevent a fall

Sap oozing from the veins
In the open wound
Makes its way
Toward the earth

Ants and wasps gather
To feast on sweetness
The tree's misfortune
Their delight

Winter Trees

Winter trees
against the gray december sky
lift bare and boney arms up high
while through their icy fingers shrills
a northern wind that bites and chills

Winter trees
stark silhouettes that loom so tall
against the glowing western wall
within their crooks bear robins' nests
though void of last spring's chirping guests

Winter trees
whose roots reach deep into the earth
draw up the water of rebirth
that will through trunk and branches run
and give us respite from the sun.

Judith Barban

The Killdeer

I saw a killdeer on her nest
in the middle of a railroad track
black bands around her neck and chest
brown wings resting on her back

tiny eggs beneath her beating heart
in the warmth of cover
safe within the rampart—
the body of their mother

their fragile home of twigs and sticks
laid among the ties and steel
surrounded by houses of mortar and bricks
seemed so natural and genteel

I couldn't help but wonder
if she would up and fly
when iron wheels of thunder
shaking the rails came roaring by

silly bird why did you use
this dangerous space
could you not choose
a safer place?

IV
Imperfect Stones:
Fake, Flawed, and Fractured

Carousel

"Come on," they say, "it's fun!"
The music is gay,
lights turn and burn,
and everyone is smiling.
So I choose a noble horse
holding high his golden mane,
and sit upon his back.
He slowly takes me round at first,
then a little faster.
Gaining speed, more and more,
faces blur, noises fuse,
misgiving turns to fear.
In terror I grab my stallion's neck,
in horror touch his eyes of glass.

The Cabin

In a frosty cabin
hidden in the glen
a woman sits alone.

One plate on the table,
one chair before the fire,
one coat beside the door.

A steamy pot of stew
simmering on the stove,
her solitary meal.

With bended back she stands
and walks across the room,
as bones and floor woods crack.

Her blue and wrinkled hand
fragile as the night
rocks an empty cradle.

Judith Barban

I Knew What You Were Going to Say

I knew what you were going to say
that late November night
when we stood by the frozen lake
my throat knotted like barbed wire
front teeth digging into my lower lip

you spoke in short phrases
swallowing between them
the words came forth
in frosty vapors from your mouth
entered my ears
plunged downward as crystals shards
striking the surface of my heart

your face was hard, jaw set
eyes looking straight out
over the blank whiteness
seeing nothing but the effort of speech
you stopped
and in the wintry silence
clouds like thin gray hopes
vanished in the clearing sky
the moon shone down its steady stone
and we could not move nor speak
but stood listening
to the cracking of the setting ice.

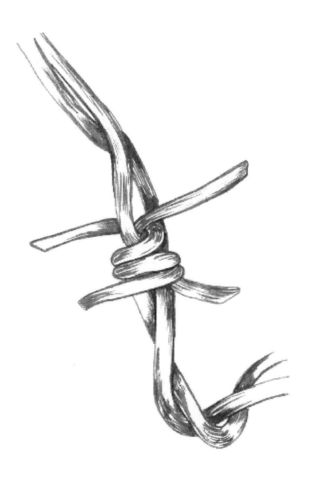

Throw-Away

use Them
get inured to Them
tire of Them
grow bored with Them
find Them disgusting

rags
newspapers
clothes
jewelry
furniture
houses
jobs
husbands
wives
parents
a child

once interested in Them
once delighted by Them
once enjoyed Them
once proud of Them
once loved Them

put Them in the trash
toss Them out
care no more about Them
forget Them
let somebody else have Them

throw Them away

Streaks

a raindrop blown against the window
makes one silver on the glass
a comet passing by the Earth
makes one cloudy in the night
a tire too quickly braked
makes one smudgy on the street

jets put white ones in the air
age puts gray ones in my hair
tears put wet ones on my cheeks

your words last night
left a black one
across my heart

Promises

your promises became
a garment
worn so thin I could
see through it

more time together
more dinners out
clothes that
didn't come from
the thrift shop
a vacation

in the waiting
hope grew thin too
until it became
a hole where
there was no more
of you

Who You Are

you left—
a stallion
rearing up
head high
eyes defiant
hooves thrashing

you returned—
a puppy
repentant
tail low
head down
eyes begging

forgiveness

don't you know
you are
neither
horse
nor
dog

The South Side of Crete
Summer 1968

We pick up the VW camper in London
travel the British Isles sleeping amid
ruined castles and fields of sheep
then ferry to the coast of France

On the continent we consult
the Europa Camping guide
and find a crowd of poor students
like ourselves seeing the world

From the heel of Italy's boot
we sail for Greece and her islands—
the ultimate odyssey for our age
to find our western roots

Corfu, Delos, Mykanos, Crete
we drive alone through the valley
of windmills, stopping to buy wine
and pluck wild figs for breakfast

The deserted beach of the southern side
sprawls before us in unrelenting sun
the Aegean cools our burning skin
refreshes our road-weary soul

At night we lie beneath a billion
stars—mentioning the names
of some and pointing out constellations
the Milky Way a streaming cloud above us

Awakened by the morning we go
in search of water
to slake our thirst
and clean ourselves of salt and sand

We stop at a well in the midst
of a vineyard "Nero, parakalo,"
we ask of the old man
he drenches us with buckets of water

Standing there at the apex of our youth
we could not possibly know
that *we* would vanish like the stars
of a black and profound night

you would follow the way of the sand
and I the way of the sun

Heart

I never noticed you there
hidden darkly in your cage
I took you for granted
paying you no mind
until you started bumping
fluttering all around
they told me you were sick
never would get well
I'd better take good care
without you I cannot live at all
I was so unaware

your chambers now are my concern
I listen all the time
even in my sleep
I hear your measured cadence
you are the very core of me
I was so late to learn

V
Costume Jewelry:
Play is the Thing

Woman in Morning Meditation

Try to clear your mind
must do laundry

Try to clear your mind
have to buy groceries

Try to clear your mind
house needs dusting

Try to clear your mind
forgot to clean litter pan

Try to clear your mind
bug man comes at ten

Try to clear your mind
water house plants

Try to clear your mind
soccer practice carpool

Try to clear your mind
gas up the van

Try to clear your mind
write checks tonight

Try to clear your mind
he'll want sex

* * *

Mind cleared

Limericks

There was a poor horse from New Guinea
Whose breeders did think him too skinny.
But once with a mare
He had such a flare,
For miles you could hear her gay whinny.

A lady who lived in Bangor
Never entered a barroom before.
She sat on a stool
And felt like a fool,
Drank one, then ordered two more.

I once knew a man named O'Neal
Who met a young girl from Mobile.
When he got her to wed
And jumped in her bed,
She told him quite simply, "No deal!"

There was a young fiddler named Burt
Who never would put on a shirt.
He played with great zest
Upon a bare chest
And kept all his listeners alert.

I once knew a man named Andy
Whose wife ate lots of candy.
She became so wide
That she finally died,
And he said "That's just fine and dandy."

A poet whose name was McCord
O'er sonnets and limericks poured.
But with rhymes inharmonious
And rhythms erroneous
He never could win an award.

Eve's Recipe for Revenge

Rip off the stem
Rough up the skin
Ram in the stick
Plunge the sweet thing
Head first
Not once, not twice,
But three times
In boiling caramel sauce

Anxiety

you are there
waiting for me
when i wake
you keep me
moving slowly
make me hesitate
i'm accustomed to
the way you sap
all color from my life
wrap me in
your gloomy cloak
fill my mind with dread
my chest with fear

sometimes watching a movie
or reading a good book
you disappear for a while
my heart slows down
i manage a smile
but you're back
if the phone rings
and always at "the end"

my constant companion
i know you would like
to sleep with me
accompany my dreams
but beside my bed
there is a true friend
mightier than you
before i turn out the light
i swallow the little pink pill

Caribbean Island

I wish I were on a
Caribbean island

sitting on the beach
watching the waves
listening to their muted thunder

hearing the crackle
of the dried palmleaf parasol
responding to ocean breezes

ice in the mai tai clinking
against the glass as I place it
on the table beside me

somewhere behind me
the sound of steel drums
playing island tunes
in a soft-patterned rhythm
makes the heart dance

I feel the company
of young laughter from the
open air bar
it makes me smile

I keep smiling while
taking the kids' jeans
out of the washer
swaying from side to side
I put them in the dryer

Young People

I think teenagers are way so cool
they hang around malls
and learn to drive
I can't wait to be a teen

I think twenty is old
they actually buy things in malls
they want to get married
I'm glad I'm a teen

I think thirty is old
their dances are dumb
their language is dated
I'm glad I'm twenty

I think forty is old
they talk about their kids
have savings accounts
I'm glad I'm thirty

I think fifty is old
they worry about the future
count down to retirement
I'm glad I'm forty

I think sixty is old
they're a little slow
to understand jokes
I'm glad I'm fifty

I think seventy is old
they have knees and
hips replaced
I'm glad I'm sixty

I think eighty is old
they use walkers
in assisted-living places
I'm glad I'm seventy

I think ninety is way so cool
childish eyes and smiles
shine through wrinkled faces
I can't wait to be ninety

A Bar of Soap in the Shower

nice shape oval tapered
pretty color pink rosy
pleasant smell clean fresh
lots of suds frothy
slipping out of my hand
sliding around my feet
bending to pick it up
hair getting wet
water in my eyes
can't find it
have it now
squooshed away
squooshed away again
stepped on it
fell on my hip
hip hurting
maybe broken
dial 911
Dial???

VI
Crowns of Glory:
The Lord their God will save them on that day. . .
They will sparkle like jewels in a crown.
Zechariah 9.16

Sacred Lament

With silver moonstrings
I enlace your feet
You step into the shadow

With gossamer wings
I hover over you
You brush me away

With a fountain of color
I bathe your eye
You ignore my beauty

With exotic incense
I enchant your nostrils
You forget my fragrance

With harmonious sounds
I delight your ear
You do not hear my voice

With fruit of the vine
I refresh your mouth
You have no taste for me

With tender breezes
I caress your skin
You cannot feel my presence

What if I should die for you
Would you love me then?

Death on the Cross Road

A deer stood in the jogging path
that runs beside the crossroad.
Hesitant, she sniffed the air,
then bounded forth with *grace*.

A deer lies in the jogging path
that runs beside the crossroad.
Slender legs, stiff and straight,
protrude from the *gentle* body
fed on garden flowers.
Eyes wide, ears erect,
no broken bones.

An early-morning runner
slacks his pace and stops
beside the hapless doe.
Circling, he stares, not knowing
why, or what to do.
He backs away, turns,
continues his way
with slower step
and *lowered head.*

A deer lies in the jogging path
that runs beside the crossroad.
A stream of *blood and water*
flows from her *perfect* nose.

Shadows

memories
are like
our own
shadows

facing the morning Sun
they are
behind us
we can't see them

we stand
on top of them
in the full Sun
of noon

our back to the late Sun
they are
before us
lengthy and lean

as long as we are
in the Light
there will be
shadows
until we ourselves
become
shadows

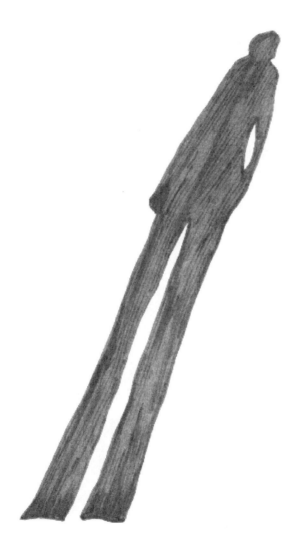

Fishing Lessons

Fishing is a trip into the unknown
what's down there beneath the surface?
rocks? weeds? a bass? a pike?
but knowing what you want to hook

Fishing involves handling equipment
choosing the right line weight
filling the reel
assembling everything properly

Fishing develops special skills
tying on a leader or lure
tying two lines together
aiming your cast with exactness

Fishing teaches quick response
to set the hook
to release the fish
getting out of a snag

Fishing increases patience
willing to wait
to try different bait
believing in what you can't see

Fishing is transcendent
meditation with no thoughts
focusing primarily on
the end of the line

Searching

Who can know the mind of God
to think as the Omniscient thinks
to see past present and future
as one and the same

Who can even try
to explain the Omnipotent
creator of the infinitely
great and small

How can we find
the invisible
the inaudible
albeit Omnipresent

Your Hands

your hands
are tiny hands
clasped in mine
smooth, tender
clumsy, wet hands
you are my child

your hands
are strong hands
clasped in mine
sure, hard
firm, devoted hands
you are my husband

your hands
are gentle hands
clasped in mine
sharing, caring
laughing, wise hands
you are my sister

your hands
are hard-working hands
clasped in mine
wrinkled, loving
warm, healing hands
you are my mother

your hands
are invisible hands
clasped in mine
powerful, giving
nail-pierced, forgiving hands
you are my God

Miracles

There have been
miracles in my life
paced apart but steady

Some a meteor
unexpected
striking hard

large, life-changing
breath-taking

Others a leaf
spiraling softly
watched, awaited

secret heartaches
a word wiped away

Undeserving of them all
I lift my eyes to the hills
and dare hope again

The Healing

I think it happened during mass.
The priest lifted the chalice
the round of unleavened bread:
"Through Him, with Him, and in Him . . ."

I played, they sang the "Amen."
We prayed the "Our Father,"
intoned the "Lamb of God."
I left the piano and went forward
to receive,
to receive the wafer and the wine,
to receive my silent God,
my silent, omnipotent God.

Mama

I have seen Him in a face
whose eyes radiant with love
and smile of gentle grace
bring the gift of joy

I have heard Him in a voice
like a cooling stream
that slakes the heart's thirst
teaches the wisdom of laughter

I have felt Him in a presence
more potent than any medicine
just to know "She is here!"
imparts hope and healing

I have watched Him in a life
of sacrifice and selfless tears
shining with heaven's beauty
and love beyond measure

When that day comes, face to His face
I will recognize a friend
an old familiar warmth
for I have known Him, Mama, in you

You are . . .

You are everything I wished for
loving, gentle, kind and wise
your presence makes me smile

You are the love of my life
I tried so many others
that left me unfulfilled

You are my knight in shining armor
who rescued me from the danger
of following the crowd, the fads

You are my guidance counselor
helping me make decisions
that always turn out right

You are the one I kook up to
admiring your strength
your firmness of purpose

You are my hope for the future
you've planned it out for me
made me feel secure

You are my comfort
when things go wrong
or people are unkind

You are always there for me
no matter what I need
you find a way to provide

You are my source of joy
my bright spot in the dark
you wipe away my tears

You are the way
I want to follow

You are the truth
I need to know

You are the light
that gives me life

You are I AM

Judith Barban

Trying

all sermons spoken
all hymns sung
all rhymes written
try to describe You

all prayers uttered
all cries raised
all hopes whispered
try to reach You

all heads bowed
all knees bent
all hands raised
try to worship You

all verses read
all psalms repeated
all scriptures studied
try to understand You

all tears shed
all penance done
all confessions made
try to appease You

all seems in vain
all falls short
all ends in silence
perhaps trying is enough

Morning Star Rising
2 Peter 1.19

Morning Star
rising

rising from pain
rising from sorrow
rising from guilt

rising into repentance
rising into forgiveness
rising into joy

Morning Star
shining, a diadem
crowning my heart

shining in truth
shining in beauty
shining in love
shining in death

Notes

In prose fiction and poetry the reality behind the work is almost always transformed and re-created.

Crowns

Inspired by a seminar on poetry taught by poet Dana Wildsmith at the 2009 Southeastern Writers' Workshop, St. Simons Island, GA. Once an amateur actress, I have played many roles. And so, too, in life. "But the greatest of these is love," 1 Corinthians 13.13.

Love in the Sixties I

As a would-be "hippy" in the late 60's, I hung around the "make-love-not-war" long hairs. Much of what I experienced during those days informs not only this poem but a number of others.

Love in the Sixties II

References to several pop songs by the Beatles.

Soul Music

An old hymnbook with "shaped notes"—a type of musical notation introduced in the early 19th century to facilitate singing— brought me consolation during a period of heartbreak.

Between

The idea for this poem came from a famous map, "La Carte du Tendre," in the 17th-century French novel *Clélie* by Mlle de Scudéry. At pretentious high-aristocracy gatherings (the *précieux*) it provoked discussions of the nature and course of love.

If

An effort to delineate the philosophy of the early hippy movement. The title is drawn from the pop-rock song written by David Gates in 1971 and popularized by his group known as Bread.

On the Beach

My husband and I spend time every year at our favorite spot in the Carolinas, Sunset Beach, NC, a non-commercial family beach. I am always reminded of my childhood days in the 40's when my family vacationed at Folly Beach, near Charleston, SC.

High School Reunion
    Decatur (GA) High, class of 1957.

Sitting on the Porch Sipping Ice Tea
    A personal ritual at our home in Tega Cay. The best way to relax and enjoy memories—and summertime in the South.

Daddy
    Raised on a farm outside Manning, SC, Daddy was a quiet, hard-working man who served in France during World War I. He held positions as a policeman on the beat (Blackville, SC), railroad detective, and—the job he most loved—a Federal revenue agent catching moonshiners in the mountains of north Georgia.

Claire
    One of two older sisters. Six years my senior, she was, and still is, my Muse.

Road Trips
    Our annual trips to Folly Beach in a blue '41 Ford. No air conditionning.

Getting a New Dog
    Chips died in 2005. We did not get another dog, but adopted a stray black-and-white tuxedo cat we named Steinway.

Three Christmas Trees
    An award-winning poem, Southeastern Writers' Workshop, 2012. Memories of childhood and first-marriage Christmases. The final line was suggested by Victor Hugo's poem "Demain dès l'aube . . .".

Family Reunion
    The instant bond I had with this child is still with me today although I never saw her again.

There Was a Time
    The innocence of childhood in Atlanta, GA.

Seasonal Haiku
 1st place award for poetry, Southeastern Writers' Workshop, 2009. The result of an on-line creative writing course assignment.

The Locusts of Summer in the South
 We would find the locust shells clinging to the trunk of two oak trees in the backyard. I remember being afraid of them, thinking they contained the ghosts of their former tenants. And I remember the haunting sound of their songs.

The Killdeer
 An actual sighting on the tracks by Cedar Street in Rock Hill, SC.

I've Learned and **Feeder Wars**
 After forty years of labor in education, I have begun to observe the here-to-fore neglected things around me.

The Virus
 Written during the course of a six-week battle with the flu.

Out West
 A "Scenic Parks Explorer" Trafalgar tour with my husband, September 2011.

The Summer of No Sun
 June, July, August 2013. Very little sun.

Sea Poem
 See "On the Beach"

Dirge
 Composed the day I learned I had a heart problem. It seemed to sap the beauty out of life or rather the life out of life.

Winter Trees
 An exercise in traditional poetic form. Here rhymed couplets are set in iambic tetrameter.

Carousel
An earlier version of this poem dates from my "hippy period."

The Cabin
1st Place Award, Southeastern Writers' Workshop, 2010. Perhaps a reflection of time spent in remote fishing outposts in the Canadian wilderness. Or simply an effort to capture the psychological and physiological effects of loneliness. See Judith Shulevitz, "The Lethality of Loneliness," *The New Republic*, May 27, 2013.

Heart
See "Dirge"

Throw Away
In 1994 Susan Smith, a 40-year-old mom, strapped her two sons, ages 3 and 1, in her car and drove it into a lake in Union County, SC. Her claim that she was a victim of car-jacking proved false. Her boyfriend had rejected her because he didn't want children. She threw them away. And there are many similar stories.

I Knew What You Were Going to Say
Outside Iowa City, late fall 1963. I had begun work on a PhD in French at the University of Iowa.

Streaks
Fort Lauderdale, FL, January 2013.

Promises
My first husband, Richard, was and professor of English and a never-published novelist.

The South Side of Crete
Summer 1968. A *wanderyar* in Europe with Richard who later died of cancer. I remarried a brilliant concert pianist who has been the light of my life.

Eve's Recipe for Revenge
A writing assignment in poetry class, Southeastern Writers' Workshop, 2012. We were asked to write a short poem about an apple.

Woman in Morning Meditation
    My tribute to soccer moms.

Limericks
    "There was a poor horse . . ." won 1st place in the limerick contest, Southeastern Writers' Workshop, 2009.

Anxiety
    Xanax, anyone?

A Bar of Soap in the Shower
    My sister's 2' x 2' shower inspired this one no doubt.

Carribean Island
    A tribute to moms in general.

Young People
    A senior moment.

Crowns of Glory
    Visions along life's long, slow journey to find God.

Popular Fiction by Judith Barban
from ThomasMax Publishing

Poplar River

Judith Barban

Karen Kingsley and her husband have been given a honeymoon trip to Poplar River in the Canadian wilderness by her husband's cousin, Bobby. Karen immediately finds herself at home in the wild and develops into an expert fisherwoman who looks forward to returning to Poplar River. But all is not well with Karen, despite the birth of a daughter and musical skills that bring her more offers than she can accept. She loses twin sons, then finds her husband mysteriously depressed. In a sort-of reverse *Dr. Doolittle*, Karen's encounters with the animals of Poplar River are first told through her eyes, then through the eyes of the animals who tell their sides of the stories. From ThomasMax Publishing, $13.95 in print, $5.99 in Kindle or Nook e-book format.

Meredith's Wolf

Judith Barban

When Meredith Marsten's floatplane loses power in a storm, the 16-year-old Canadian bush pilot is forced to land on an unknown lake isolated in the wilderness of northern Manitoba, Canada. Realizing that the lake is the very one where she and her step-father had released her now-grown wolf pup back into the wild, Meredith embarks on a quest to reunite with her beloved "Wolfie." Thus she begins a suspenseful journey through the pristine boreal forest, a journey full of encounters with the drama of nature, animals, humans, and her own surprising destiny. From ThomasMax Publishing, $12.95 in print, $4.99 in Kindle or Nook e-book format.

CPSIA information can be obtained at www.ICGtesting.com
Printed in the USA
LVOW08s0022210414

382501LV00002B/5/P

9 780991 433209